What people are sa

Pray Then Listen

Teresa's book on how to talk to God flows from her experience of prayer as a two-way conversation. Mixed with everyday examples, she practically shares how to live a life seasoned with prayer. Providing foundational frameworks for prayer in the different seasons of life, this book will help us all move deeper in our relationship with God.

Andy Frost, Share Jesus International

This is a wonderfully open, generous, and personal account of Teresa's journey with God and her relationship with Him through prayer and the power of the Holy Spirit. It is really encouraging and helpful to anyone wishing to deepen their relationship with Christ.

Madeleine Walters, Director of Diocesan Evangelisation Commission, RC Archdiocese of Cardiff

This is a very necessary book for our time. Research on intentional disciples shows that a key tool to help the majority of Catholics to move from merely belonging to actively believing is testimony of what it's really like to have a relationship with Jesus. Teresa does what few people do and writes openly about her inner life. Our generation needs witnesses like her.

Rev Fr Gareth Leyshon, Director of Adult Religious Education, RC Archdiocese of Cardiff

I think this book is wonderful. Teresa has given a very honest exposé of her prayer life and written a real, easy and ready to read guide to prayer, knowing that this will lead to people having a deeper personal relationship with Jesus.

Sue Brice, Licenced Lay Minister

In her book *Pray Then Listen: A heart-to-heart with God* Teresa O'Driscoll explores the art of conversation with God in prayer. She shares her prayer journey in order to help others – a call she felt drawn to fulfil, sharing her many tried and tested methods of prayer formulated over the years. Yet she encourages her readers not just to follow, but to make a concerted effort to make their prayer life a personal one. Teresa shows us how, in purity of heart, we can approach our Heavenly Father – the beauty of this book being its simplicity and childlike innocence. This book is a reminder that Our Father always wants His children to turn to Him in good times and bad. Teresa offers prayers for a wide variety of occasions. Anyone reading this will develop, not just an authentic prayer life, but a close, deep personal relationship with the Holy Trinity. You will learn from this to carry God with you in every moment in all life's ups and downs. I can't recommend this book highly enough.

Kathy Bishop, Founder and editor-in-chief of *The Faith Companion*

Previous books

Non-fiction

9 Days to Heaven: How to Make Everlasting Meaning of Your Life
Published by O Books ISBN 9781905047734

9 Days to Heaven: How to Make Everlasting Meaning of Your Life
e-book
Published by O Books ISBN 9781780999364

Other books
Fiction

*Angel at the Paradise Hotel: Because even on vacation personal
demons tag along*
Published by Roundfire Books ISBN 9781789048858

*Angel at the Paradise Hotel: Because even on vacation personal
demons tag along* e-book
Published by Roundfire Books ISBN 9781789048865

Pray Then Listen

A heart-to-heart with God

Pray Then Listen

A heart-to-heart with God

Teresa O'Driscoll

CIRCLE
BOOKS

Winchester, UK
Washington, USA

JOHN HUNT PUBLISHING

First published by Circle Books, 2022
Circle Books is an imprint of John Hunt Publishing Ltd., No. 3 East St., Alresford,
Hampshire SO24 9EE, UK
office@jhpbooks.com
www.johnhuntpublishing.com
www.circle-books.com

For distributor details and how to order please visit the 'Ordering' section on our website.

Text copyright: Teresa O'Driscoll 2021

ISBN: 978 1 78904 369 3
978 1 78904 370 9 (ebook)
Library of Congress Control Number: 2021942238

A CIP catalogue record for this book is available from the British Library.

Scripture quotations are from the Revised Standard Version published by HarperCollins
Publishers, copyright © 1989 by the Division of Christian education of the National Council
Churches of Christ in the USA, and are used by permission. All rights reserved.

Design: Stuart Davies

UK: Printed and bound by CPI Group (UK) Ltd, Croydon, CR0 4YY
US: Printed and bound by Thomson Shore, 7300 West Joy Road, Dexter, MI 48130

We operate a distinctive and ethical publishing philosophy in
all areas of our business, from our global network of authors to
production and worldwide distribution.

Contents

This book is dedicated to Charlotte and Tom, my late mother and father – gone to join the angels but always in my heart, until we meet again…

Speak, Lord, for thy servant is listening. **1 Samuel 3:10**

Preface

Hello and welcome,

I presume that, as you have been drawn to this book, you want to feel more of Christ's loving support in your daily challenges. If you are one of the many turning to Christianity for the first time to get answers in this sometimes frightening world, then, by God's grace, you will find them using my methods. These are simple, easy, and often relaxing, and can be adapted to fit perfectly to your own life.

No matter where you are right now in your walk with God, I show you how to speak to Him from your heart and to listen expectantly for His reply.

Writing as I am in the middle of the Covid-19 coronavirus pandemic, this testing situation has been a reminder of just how much we need God. Consider that God made us to know Him, love Him and serve Him in this world, and to be with Him in the next. Being mindful of His promise that this life is only the starting point of Eternity with Him, keeps everything in perspective. The bonus is that, an active awareness of Christ's company boosts confidence – lightening and brightening your life.

Years ago I chose to bring God into everyday living – as I show you in the book. As you learn to trust Him as I do, and to rely on *His* strength to see you through, you will be able to cope with everything life throws at you. You will discover in these pages that I mean this in a real and practical sense, not just a theoretical, theological one. If you make the same choice to put *your* trust in Christ, it will fill you with resilience and hope.

Before closing I want to say a big thank you to Spiro Sueref for his inspirational, selfless ministry of prayer and healing. I thank him also for his very kind evaluation of this book in his Foreword.

Teresa O'Driscoll

April 2021

Foreword

Pray Then Listen is not just a basic guide to prayer, it is potentially a life-changing challenge for anyone who reads it, as it provokes us to reflect on, and recollect, our own behaviour and decisions in the light and presence of our merciful God. Drawing us to biblical teachings and principles, it steers us into the realm of both the nature of God and the true nature of Christians.

This is truly a book that encourages and coaches the reader along to discover the way of having a meaningful, heartfelt relationship with God through prayer. Teresa does this without holding anything back: she draws the reader into her own spiritual journey and discovery of God, who wants to dialogue with us in our everyday life.

As someone who was drawn by the Holy Spirit to prayer, and then to lead a prayer group for nearly twenty years, the journey for me continues as I discover the ongoing love and patience of God as he tirelessly guides us to come to know him deeper and deeper.

Teresa addresses this nicely and cleverly as though we are sitting with her having a chat over coffee. She moves us into her life's ups and downs, her personal experiences and challenges, and shows how, even in her lowest and darkest moments and experiences, God was there to help her up again through prayer.

No doubt this would make a great book to give to someone who is starting off at prayer, as well as the experienced prayer warrior, as it could be used as a reference book for prayers.

It is also a great evangelizing tool. And a testimony of God's love and goodness, and the power working in Teresa's life of prayer, when God is the goal and the focus.

Teresa brings her charm and wit as well as her experience into life in this wonderful book and I would recommend having this book close at hand for daily prayer and meditation. Enjoy it!

Spiro Sueref
Prayer Group Leader
St Peter's Prayer Group Cardiff
28 November, 2020

Acknowledgements

Heartfelt thanks to my dear friend Brigid Kelly who helped me with the subtitle of the book quite soon before going to join the angels…

Thanks to Brett Syson – the first person I showed the book to – for your encouragement and friendship.

Thanks to other friends including fellow Christian writer Pauline Lewis, and brilliant artist Toni Ndikanwu and his wife Margarita.

Big thanks also to friends Susan Bruno, Gilly Charlemagne, Erica Evans, Joanie Gritsopoulos, Renée and Robert Killian-Dawson, Zeffie Klironomou, Dianne Microutsicos, Artemis Pappas, Janet Parkinson, Sophia Periclakes, Mary Taylor, and Dimitris Zissimopoulos. And to 'the girls': Sandra Hill, Janet Motto, and Kath Wilks, and also Beverly Lawrence – with the angels but always in our hearts.

A big thank you to Canon William Isaac and Dr James Campbell for your help with the Imprimatur application – even though it was eventually deemed unnecessary for this work.

Thanks also go to my highly talented singer/songwriter brother Kenny Driscoll for being there.

Finally, I want to say a big thank you to my publisher John Hunt for his continued trust in my work, and to Dominic James at John Hunt Publishing Ltd for his crucial part in this publication.

Section One

Introduction

God Wants to Talk to You!

I have it on good authority that God wants to be part of your daily life. He said to me on 15 January, 2017 (my father's birthday), **+ "Write a book and show people how to speak to Me."** Later, it became clear that Jesus wants you to talk to Him in a way that lets Him speak back. This book, then, is a prayer guide which shows you how to do just that.

If you are already a practising Christian it is for use alongside your current devotions and formal prayers which have, I hope, been sustaining you throughout your life. It is definitely NOT a substitute for them. If though, this is all unfamiliar to you it can lead you gently into a new life in the company of Christ, Who will then show you the next steps.

In the book I share the many prayers I have formulated over the years, to act as a signpost guiding you towards praying with your *own* words. These words, spoken from your heart, can let Jesus speak to you from His heart. Through this empowering Divine connection, as you bring Him your questions, problems, and dilemmas, His input can benefit every aspect of your life.

I must say immediately that I am not a holy person or any more special than you (we are all special to God though) but at some point in the distant past I began to speak to Him informally and to listen for His guidance. So, when He asked me to write the book it was not unusual to hear from Him. But He had never made such a request before.

To be clear, I need to explain that when God spoke, I did not hear these words with my ears, rather, the words came into my mind and touched my heart. But they were definitely not *my* words.

As Christians we are all encouraged to have a close personal relationship with Jesus. But that is often easier said than done.

As with a lot of things, most of us were not born knowing how to do this. It is something to be learned. For me, it took that change to informal dialogue – which I share with you in the book.

I hope that as you read and practise my way of speaking to Christ, and begin to develop your *own* way, your *own* words, it enlivens your whole life – starting with deeper meaning and appreciation of your regular worship and prayers.

This is a journey so where do we start? Or, more specifically, where do YOU start?

The answer to that is: You start from wherever you are in your life right now. Mark the beginning of this momentous journey by carrying out the following 3-step meditation.

Meditation

Step 1.
Take a deep breath. Breathe out slowly and relax.

Step 2.
Consider that everything in your life has led up to this moment. Undoubtedly the Holy Spirit is prompting you to draw closer to your Maker.

Step 3.
Underline this by saying – either aloud or in your head – the following sentence: "I want to feel closer to You, Lord." And with that verbalized desire your new spiritual journey has begun.

Note

Throughout the book, in relation to God, I capitalize Him, He, and so on. This is my personal choice, though this method is not as widespread as formerly used. The Bible quotes though, from the Revised Standard Version, do not have this capitalization.

Tip

Having a Bible (*any* authorized version is fine) close by, to view quotes in their context as you work through the book, can strengthen the whole experience.

Meditation

You have just undertaken the first of many meditations you will find in the book. If you have never meditated before, you now know how simple it can be.

A dictionary definition of "meditate" goes something like this: "Meditate – 1. Focus one's mind for a period of time for spiritual purposes or as a method of relaxation. 2. Think carefully about something."

Actually, my simple meditations can be said to encompass all three aspects. Through focus on breathing you relax and turn your thoughts – however briefly – away from daily concerns and onto Christ.

❖ **Meditation can create an oasis of calm in a trying day**

Each meditation in the book has a handful or less of steps and you can take as long or as short a time as you want to carry them out. For instance, I did the above 3-steps in about 30 seconds. Yes, really! And I did sincerely focus on the subject. But you may have taken a minute or longer.

There is no right or wrong length of time for a meditation. It really depends on you and how much time you have, or want to take on each one. You may sometimes even want to turn this, or any meditation in the book, into a whole day of contemplation. Going deeper into the topic and pondering on it with God's company. And you could carry this out with a group of like-minded friends.

As you make your journey through the book if, say, a particular prayer resonates with you and your circumstances and it is not already set into a meditation you could turn it into one yourself using my step method.

❖ **Meditation is a great way to invite a heart-to-heart with God**

Finally, I recommend taking a relaxing breath frequently as you make your spiritual journey with prayers and other daily activities. As I hope you have discovered – through using Step 1 in the meditation above – it is an incredibly powerful method of quickly reducing tension (which we are often unaware of) and of clearing the mind so that we can do our best in all situations, which is what God wants of us.

Section One Overview

- God wants you to speak to Him in a way that lets Him talk back.

- Draw closer to Christ by opening your heart to Him.

- Use meditation to talk things over with Jesus.

Section Two

The Two-Way Street of Prayer

What Is Prayer?

Before we take one more step let us look at what prayer is. Consulting, again, a dictionary, which necessarily defines the commonly understood meaning of the word, we find a description like this: "Prayer – a solemn request for help or expression of thanks to God."

In other words: please help me and thank you.

Gosh! How bald. How narrow.

Yet, it may well be your own interpretation of prayer.

I would rather define prayer as a form of communication which a dictionary defines something like this: "Communication – the means of sending or receiving information."

Read that and ponder upon it. The seemingly subtle difference in defining prayer holds within it the key to profound exchanges with God. Because in all likelihood, He'll have something to say back to you. If only you give Him the chance!

❖ Please give God a chance to talk back

It is a strong possibility that, until today, you have addressed God mainly with formal prayers. These are, and will remain, the foundation of your faith and worship, as they do mine.

❖ Formal worship and prayer are irreplaceable

Now though, I want to build on those formal prayers by opening things out; a lot! This, then, is the essence of the whole book. And even if you find the experience a little strange at first, I hope that you are eager to try it out.

Before you go on though, I want to highlight a very important aspect of any kind of prayer, be it formal or informal: Jesus tells us to pray with confidence and trust in His loving response.

Therefore I tell you, whatever you ask in prayer, believe that you have received it, and it will be yours.
Mark 11:24

And so, as you work your way through the prayers in the book, always approach God with faith.

Note

Before praying formally, I usually begin with the Sign of the Cross prayer, and perhaps you do too. Often, I say this prayer on its own – such as when I hear unsettling news, or good news, or whatever, and quickly want to bring God into the situation. With the prayers I am going to share with you in the following pages of the book, I often begin them with the Sign of the Cross prayer too.

In case you are not familiar with this method, but want to try it, I have outlined it for you below.

Say the following prayer while sketching out the shape of the Cross, on which Jesus died for us, with your right hand. As you say Line One: touch your fingers to your forehead. As you say Line Two: bring your fingers down to touch your middle. As you say Line Three: touch your fingers to your left shoulder, then right shoulder. And as you say the Amen, finish off by putting your hands together briefly in the prayer position.

Prayer: Sign of the Cross
Line One: In the name of the Father
Line Two: And of the Son
Line Three: And of the Holy Spirit.
Amen.

If you use the prayer to start another you could keep your hands in the prayer position throughout and finish praying with a second Sign of the Cross.

In Greece, where I lived for many years, the people sketch this Sign of the Cross in a slightly different way and do so quickly three times. They do this – as I do – on many different occasions. For instance, when riding the tram, bus or train you always know when a church is close by as passengers make their crosses. And when I added mine too I often felt that we, though strangers, experienced camaraderie from our shared love of Christ.

I wonder if you are prepared to stand up for Christ publicly in this way. As well as using this prayer you could also wear a cross, say, on a chain around your neck, or as a lapel pin. It is a practice I embraced many years ago and I love to see others wearing theirs too as it silently speaks volumes.

How do you know that God is listening?

You want to talk with God – to begin to pour your heart out in order to share your life with Him – but before doing so you really need to trust that He is listening. So how do you know that He *is* listening? Well, we can believe that because, for one thing, Jesus promised to do that.

> *If a man loves me, he will keep my word, and my Father will love him, and we will come to him and make our home with him.*
> **John 14:23**

So there we have it. God lives with us.

God lives with *you*!

It therefore follows that, perhaps you don't yet have as close a personal relationship with Him as you could, because, you often ignore His presence. Now there is a sobering thought.

Definitely a cue for a prayer!

Prayer for forgiveness

Dear Lord,

I am so sorry for all the times I have ignored You. As You promise to live with me, so I promise to try to remember that.

I ask Your help to do this in Jesus' name. Amen.

Note

I end each and every prayer request in Jesus' name because He asked us to do so.

Whatever you ask in my name, I will do it, that the Father may be glorified in the Son.
John 14:13

Following this instruction is therefore a crucial part of prayer requests.

Make a fresh start to your life

I am a huge fan of Fresh Starts! They are very powerful and freeing. Deliberately acknowledging that, though you may have lingering regrets about some aspects of your past, it is impossible to change anything.

Facing that squarely you can choose today to do things differently. Instead of going it alone you can carry things out with the help of the Holy Spirit.

Take a few moments to embrace this important new decision by undertaking the following 4-step meditation.

Meditation

Step 1.
Take a deep breath. Breathe out slowly and relax.

Step 2.
Now consider your willingness to undertake this new beginning.

Step 3.
Feel enthusiasm rising in your spirit like a stream of cleansing, healing water as you say the following prayer.

Prayer for a fresh start

Dear Lord Jesus,
I stand at the foot of Your cross to bring before You all my sins.
[Pause for a few moments to reflect on what you have done or have failed to do, so that you can tell Him specific things that you regret.]
I am sorry for each and every one of them.
I ask now for Your forgiveness.
I also ask that, when I have Your forgiveness, You will help

me to forgive *myself*, and in so doing set me free for a fresh start to my life.

I ask this through the same Christ our Lord. Amen.

Step 4.

Pause for a few moments and listen expectantly for anything that Christ may want to say to you now. As you go about your day keep open to His communications, which, in my experience, are often very quiet and gentle – so you will need to pay attention. As you diligently practise listening for God's guidance it will become more obvious to you.

Note

From time to time in the following pages you will meet with [Square Brackets] as you have in the above prayer. This denotes an opportunity for you to interact with the text in a personal way.

Tip

As this fresh start to your life is paving the way to new spiritual experiences, you may find it useful to get a notebook and start to record these. You could label your notebook Spiritual Enrichment, and I will refer to it that way occasionally in the book.

Listening to God (and more about writing this book)

You arrived at this point in your life through a series of decisions. The majority of these decisions will doubtless have been minor, or seemingly minor at the time. But along the way there will also have been some major ones.

Take a few moments to think over some situations in your life using the following 4-step meditation.

Meditation

Step 1.
Take a deep breath. Breathe out slowly and relax.

Step 2.
Now think about your life briefly and the choices you made to get to this point.

Step 3.
Now ask yourself how many decisions were taken with God's guidance. Some, none, most? I ask the question because, I have come to understand that, one of the best ways of drawing closer to God is to bring Him into decision-making.

Step 4.
If you choose to bring Christ into your decision-making, tell Him that good news now.

I said in my introduction that on 15 January, 2017 God commissioned this book. + **"Write a book and show people how to speak to Me,"** He said. (Actually, though that was my dad's birthday, it was a sad old day as we had lost my mother only weeks before. So hearing from God did lift my spirits.)

Two days later, I began my task. I must tell you that I didn't really know what to write. But I prayed hard for guidance. I began by writing down the things I say to God on a regular basis. It seemed like the right thing to do, but I admit I was not one hundred per cent sure I was on the right track.

On 21 February, 2017 I turned on Premier Christian Radio (find this online here: https://www.premierchristianradio.com) and in the middle of a talk by Pastor Brian Brodersen he broke off and said, "While I remember, next week I'll be holding sessions on how to pray. The Lord told me He's having difficulty speaking to people because they don't know how to pray. And He asked me to show people how to pray."

Wow! There is my confirmation, I thought. I wrote the pastor's comments in my diary.

I carried on with my book. It went quite well but when I ran over the whole text, I knew there was more to say. After praying for more guidance I started looking through my diary and came across the note about the pastor. This time, I saw it not just as confirmation of my task but a signpost to a deeper understanding of what God wanted from me.

I prayed, and began, what I can best describe as a guidance session with God. I used the following prayer as the starter.

Prayer for guidance

Dear Lord,

You asked me to write a book to show people how to speak to You. I am very sorry that I am being so dim. Please will You show me what You really want me to write.

I ask this in the name of Jesus Christ our Lord. Amen.

I kept repeating the words, "God has difficulty speaking to people because they don't know how to pray."

Then, "Write a book and show people how to speak to Me."

This eventually came down to: "Show people how to speak to Me so I can speak to them."

Okay. Now I was on a clearer track. Prayer is actually a two-way street. But mostly, I think, people treat it as a one-way street: we talk and God listens.

So, instead of God being able to guide us through life – the good times and the bad times, and the regular small challenges – we usually don't let Him get a word in edgeways, as we Brits say.

After more prayers, I made a decision.

I would give you some details of just a few of the countless exchanges I've had with God over the years as I have asked His guidance. These would be living examples of what I said and asked, and what God said in return, or how He guided me in other ways.

After reading even this far, I think you are already becoming familiar with the way I talk to God. This though, is a step beyond that: the two-way street in action. I hope you find this useful and that it inspires you to the same two-way communication with Him.

Taking notice of God

The situations I have chosen to share are varied. Sometimes I had a dilemma. At other times I was feeling very stressed, or uncomfortable. I chose these particular examples as I thought you may identify with similar challenges in your own life – maybe at home, at work, or in relationships with loved ones.

As you will discover, even though I love God and try to stay as close to Him as I can at all times, yet I am human. I get upset, I worry, and so on. I think that you will understand this and possibly feel the same emotions when the going gets tough in *your* life.

I hope, that by highlighting these times of my vulnerability, you will feel better about your own! It is bad enough when things get a bit too much without adding guilt into the mix. You know: I love God and trust in Him so I should not feel this way. Maybe that is so but though I am working towards that goal of permanent equilibrium, I'm certainly not there yet. And actually, I doubt I will achieve that on this side of heaven...

The great thing is that we can take everything to our Heavenly Father and He will see us through – as I say repeatedly.

Gosh! How very blessed we are.

As you read the following scenarios you will see that Christ chose to communicate with me in different ways. In some of the situations He spoke to me directly. On other occasions He used different means with which to guide me. It was through experiences such as these that I was able to write quite specifically about how God guides us in general, as you will read later on.

Taking notice of God in a crisis

I have discovered that when I am in a crisis I usually just need to get through the worst day, the day when it threatens to overwhelm me.

While writing this book I had one of those crisis days. On 9 June, 2017 I felt angry and betrayed by some of those closest to me, and completely alone. I did not know how I could get through the day.

It came into my mind that I should phone my friend Mary. I did so and told her of my problem. Mary understood my anger and upset. She too highlighted that the worst thing of all was the betrayal. After talking things through, she advised me to pray about it all.

Mary was right, of course, prayer was the only way forward. I don't remember the exact words I used but my prayer went something like this.

Dear Lord,
I feel so betrayed. I feel so alone. I feel so upset.
Please help me!
I beg You this in Jesus' name. Amen.

This is what happened next.

I felt prompted to go into my kitchen. There my gaze fell, and held, upon a timetable for my local swimming pool. I thought, Hmm, great idea, Lord. It was then about 2pm and the next public session was 4pm. I would go. The plan immediately calmed me down.

I felt I should look to my left. My eyes fell, and held, upon the May issue of the *Catholic People* (official newspaper of the Archdiocese of Cardiff) which I had only glanced through. Maybe there was something in it that God wanted to tell me.

I picked it up and looked at the front page. The headline read: *New priests joining the diocese – but they face a challenge!* The report was Archbishop George Stack's homily on the subject. I started reading and found this:

> *The famous novelist Agatha Christie wrote this paragraph in her autobiography: 'Quite unexpectedly one day (I think in the middle of a maths lesson) the teacher suddenly launched forth on a speech on life and religion. All of you, she said, will pass through a time when you feel despair. If you never face despair you will never know the Christian life. To be a Christian you must accept and face the life that Christ faced and lived.*
>
> *'You must enjoy things as He enjoyed things; be as happy as He was at the marriage feast of Cana; know the peace and happiness that it means to be in harmony with God and God's will. But you must also know what it means to be alone in the Garden of Gethsemane, to feel all your friends have forsaken you, that those you love and trust have turned away from you, and that God Himself has forsaken you.*
>
> *'Hold on then to the belief that this is not the end. If you love, you will suffer, and if you do not love, you do not know the meaning of the Christian life. She then returned to her compound interest and fractions with her usual vigour.'*

A quote from Agatha Christie in a church newspaper spoken by the Archbishop and directly relevant to me at that moment! What were the chances of that? I fastened onto the words, "Hold on, this is not the end." I repeated them a few times. They gave me comfort and strength.

Once again, as always, I was amazed at how God answered my prayer for help within seconds! And He continued to help me in various ways throughout that very testing day. By the next day He had helped me back into perspective.

Thank You Lord so very much for Your help.

Taking notice of God's emphatic instruction

On Good Friday 2010 in Athens (where I was living), I was watching the film *Jesus of Nazareth* starring Robert Powell. (Many other relevant films and programmes are shown in this period. You know that the real meaning of Easter centres on Christ not chocolate when you are in Greece!)

Anyway, there I am watching the film, and it is coming up to the Crucifixion. And it was very upsetting. We were commemorating Jesus dying for us. For our sins. For our redemption. In agony. Blameless. Sinless. When all He had ever done was help, cure the sick, show compassion for the bereaved by raising the dead, and so on. And they killed Him so very cruelly.

Watching the re-enactment, I wanted to come even closer to Him and do His will more. I prayed.

Dear Lord,
When I start to work again on Tuesday, will You please remind me to ask even more for Your guidance with what You want me to write.
I ask this in the name of Jesus Christ our Lord. Amen.

No sooner was the prayer out of my mouth when the words, + **"Go home!"** hit my brain.

I was so shocked that I sank down into the sofa like a popped balloon. After a few moments of getting my breath back, I piped up, "But I didn't mean that, Lord. I meant for You to guide me even more closely in my work." I was told once more, emphatically, **"Go home!"**

The shock reverberated for about 10 days. When I woke up I felt very miserable. In the end I could not face the unhappiness. I put the idea aside for a while.

One morning in mid-July, I was writing my diary and the positive things about going back to live in the UK had begun to take root. I made the decision to move.

To travel with my cat, Charlie, he had to have a pet passport. To get that he needed an identity chip, an anti-rabies vaccination, and blood test and then came a waiting period. (At that time the process took about seven months but now is contracted to a few weeks.) So I moved us to the island of Corfu for the winter and took Charlie on the first plane of the summer season into the UK. And the rest, as they say, is history.

Thank You Lord for showing me Your will.

Taking notice of God about a small but niggling worry

On the morning of 5 March, 2011 in Corfu, I was reading *Our Daily Bread,* a daily devotional (see: www.ourdailybread.org), and got very moved when I read that Jesus alone, in Revelation 5:1–12, is worthy to open the sealed scroll which was held in God's right hand.

As I sat and thought about Jesus and His amazing works and so on, I said to Him wryly, "In the face of all this it's ridiculous that I'm worried about the cage I've ordered!" (To fly Charlie, a big Maine Coon cat, over to the UK, I had needed to order him a dog cage and thought it was going to be unmanageably huge.)

Jesus said, immediately, + **"It's about as tall as that."** Meaning the sofa.

"Oh, is it?" I said, looking at the height. I saw that it wasn't as tall as I'd feared. Phew. I relaxed quite a bit.

Then I spent some time in Jesus' presence talking to Him about a lot of things. I couldn't resist at one point though, getting up and finding a ruler to measure the height of the sofa. And, yes! Practically the exact height as the cage I'd ordered.

It was a very strong experience of Jesus' presence. It stayed with me until I went to sleep late that night.

Thank You Lord for calming me down.

Taking notice of God when wanting to do a good turn was stressful

In May 2008, I was editing a book, *Athens 4 Kids!*, on a tight deadline when my artist friend Toni Ndikanwu (he illustrated my book *9 Days to Heaven: How to Make Everlasting Meaning of Your Life* find his work on: https://www.saatchiart.com/account/artwork/84970) unexpectedly arrived. He asked me to write something for him. With a new exhibition coming up, he wanted me to make a string of the titles of his paintings into some sort of cohesion for a brochure. We had a little chat. I told him that though I was busy, I was happy to help.

After he left though, I began to feel stressed so I prayed:

Dear Lord,
I want to help Toni but You know I have the other work to complete. Will You please, therefore, help me to do this for Toni quickly and effectively.
I ask this in the name of Jesus Christ our Lord. Amen.

I sat with the piece of paper Toni had given me and in a very short time had managed to frame a poem with the assortment of titles.

The way the writing came together astounded me! There was no doubt in my mind that the poem was a product of divine guidance.

I took from that experience a formula for prayer in certain situations. I have passed this on to many people when it has seemed relevant. "Don't just ask for help," I say. "Be very specific."

Thank You Lord for Your help and guidance.

Taking notice of God during a meltdown over an article

In May 2009, I was on a tight deadline to finish editing another book: *Corfu 4 Kids!*. I was off to New York in a few days to attend a writers' conference at the Marymount Manhattan College, sitting on a panel discussion on Spirituality. When I came home I would have only a short time to finish the edit. That was all fine. But! I had an extra task in my in-tray that seemed impossible to complete.

Months before I had pitched the magazine *Insider Athens* for an article on religious tourism in Malta where I had been on a journalist trip to follow in the footsteps of Saint Paul commemorating his two-thousandth birthday. The editor had outlined what kind of article she wanted but Malta formed only a small part. Although my deadline for the piece was over a month away, I knew I had to finish it before my trip.

So, I found the email from the editor and started to make phone calls, trying to pull something together. I did not get far. For one thing, she wanted quotes from someone on Mount Athos, a holy mountain in a distant part of the country, where, in any case, only males could visit. With the pressure of editing and preparing for New York, by the evening I began to realize I couldn't write what she'd asked for.

In all the hundreds and hundreds of articles I'd written, such a thing had never happened before.

I had a meltdown.

After pacing up and down my hallway, I finally plonked myself on a chair. I sent up a fervent prayer for help then slumped back and waited.

In a short time God the Father began to speak to me like this. **+ "Remember when you were a magazine editor how pressurized it was? If someone pitched an article you will** have quickly sketched what you felt was needed."

My mind turned back the clock. Yes, I thought, that's true.

"Well, this editor will have been very busy too, and, after reading your pitch, will have just come up with suggestions from the top of her head. Nothing was cast in stone."

Aha, I thought. That did make sense but where was it leading?

God continued, "You've got a quote from the Ministry of Tourism, and you could use that, couldn't you?"

"Umm, yes," I agreed tentatively. "I suppose I could." It was a very thin quote, but a quote nonetheless.

"And you've got some quotes about religious tourism from the oldest travel agency in Athens, and you could work that together, couldn't you?"

"Oh, yes, I suppose I could do that." I was still unsure.

And God continued to speak to me very gently, like a mother to a child. I confess that I had been feeling very childlike before His help.

But when He had set out the basis of my article, I began to get fired up and then knew exactly what I would do: the further research I would make to write the article.

All this took place on a Friday. The next day I made more phone calls, and sent some emails. I got a brilliant quote from a man who belonged to the Friends of Mount Athos about what that holy place meant to him, and so on.

I finished the article and filed it before I left for New York on the Tuesday.

The piece was due to be published in August. When I spoke to the editor in September she complimented me on my article. When I saw a copy, I was very pleased with it myself – especially after all the angst! (I still have that copy.)

A few years later, I was telling my friend Janet about how God speaks to me and told her the above as an example. She was intrigued.

"Oh," she said. "So you didn't just sort of 'know' what to do? It was a conversation."

"Oh, yes, a conversation," I assured her.

"Oh, gosh," she said, sounding a bit taken aback. Since then, though, she has had her own spiritual experiences I am happy to say.

Thank You Lord for Your clarity and help.

Taking notice of God during a time of grief

In May 2018, I was taking my regular walk up the footpath on the hill just above my house in a little Welsh valley. I liked to praise God as I walked past the horse in its paddock and meandered onwards beside the field of sheep. That day though, I was grieving the recent loss of my beloved father and thankfully there was no one around to see me weeping. Suddenly I became aware of the company of Jesus and "felt" Him holding my right hand.

I carried on walking and talking to Him telling Him that I was so upset, so sad, so lost, and more. It really was a moment of deep catharsis. Each time I told Him something I waited and listened for anything He may have to tell me in return. But He didn't say anything so I just carried on spilling out my feelings.

All the while as I spoke and cried, He held my hand and so I was wiping my eyes with a tissue in my left hand. Then I finally reached the bottom-line of what I was most upset about and blurted, "I feel like an orphan!" I found that discovery quite shocking. A grown woman feeling like an abandoned child. I sobbed and sobbed.

After I calmed down I really needed both hands to mop up but I didn't want to let go of Jesus' hand and finally He spoke. + **"I will be holding your hand forever,"** He said.

Gosh!

I was so very grateful that day for His patient listening while I got to the root of my sadness. And often, since, I pause and remember His words and His promise, and knowing He is holding my hand has been a huge comfort to me on many an occasion. I regard it as an extra reminder of the continuous presence of the Holy Spirit.

Thank You so very much my dear Lord and Saviour.

Taking notice of God during an illness

In January 2020, I was in the throes of a bad case of shingles. It was on the right side of my head, forehead and eyelid, and had infected my eye too. I got lots of stabbing pains which were at their worst at night. But from the start I was offering up the discomfort to help those souls who needed it. And I also tried to make my illness a bit of a spiritual journey by joining my experience to Christ in His Passion.

One night though, I was desperate to get to sleep but couldn't. I spoke to God.

Dear Lord,
I'm not asking You to take away the illness but the doctor told me I was supposed to get a good night's sleep so I could heal. So please will You help me to get to sleep.
I ask this in Jesus' name. Amen.

Then Jesus began to instruct me on ways to get more comfortable. **+ "Put your pillows more upright and sit up,"** He said. I struggled up and did so.

Yes, that did feel a little better.

"Now change your jacket, you're too warm."

For a few days it had been very cold and I was wearing a thick bedjacket. When He said that, I realized that the night was much milder and I was too warmly dressed. I did actually have a lighter jacket close by but I was feeling ill and couldn't really muster the energy to change.

"Come on," He said encouragingly. **"It will be worth the effort."** So I sat up and in a fumbling way switched jackets.

Then I slumped back onto the plumped up pillows and realized with huge relief that I felt much more comfortable. I fell asleep quickly and slept well for some hours. And I did eventually recover.

Thank You Lord for the practical way You helped me in my hour of need.

Your turn to listen expectantly to God

After reading some of my guidance interactions with God, I hope you are encouraged to start your own, or have more of your own, with Him. Of course, God speaks back – in a variety of guises – only when He wants to. We can be sure though, that He *always* hears our prayers.

As I ponder on my countless experiences of His help over the years, I have to say that, in one way or another, He *always* finds a way to guide me. Sometimes swiftly, at other times slowly one step at a time. (Please see: **Asking God for help and guidance** below.)

Try this 3-step meditation to help you on your way.

Meditation

Step 1.
Take a deep breath. Breathe out slowly and relax.

Step 2.
Say the following prayer.

Prayer to allow God to speak

Dear Lord,
I am not worthy but will You please prompt me to create more opportunities for You to speak to me if You want to.
I ask this in Jesus' name. Amen.

Step 3.
Sit for a few moments and listen for God's voice. As you go on with your day, keep open to anything God may want to say to you.

Your experiences with Jesus will be – or are already – personal to you. I can only encourage you to invite Him more and more into everything you do because what I am describing is a loving relationship – which, as I've mentioned before, takes time and effort to establish.

You may well want to record these amazing experiences in your Spiritual Enrichment notebook.

Asking God for help and guidance

You can invite God's help and guidance on any aspect of your life and in that way you keep Him involved.

If this is all new to you, try to be crystal clear and focussed when you want to converse with Him.

Try this 4-step meditation to move forwards in your goal.

Meditation

Step 1.

Take a deep breath. Breathe out slowly and relax.

Step 2.

Put your whole attention onto talking to God by saying the following prayer.

Prayer for guidance on a specific issue

Dear Lord,

I really need your help with [tell Him the specifics]. Please guide me.

I ask this in the name of Jesus. Amen.

Step 3.

Clear your mind as much as possible and rest for a few minutes. You could visualize your favourite relaxing place such as a beach or park.

Step 4.

Put your calm focus back onto God and listen for His guidance. If He has nothing to tell you right away, go on with your day while keeping vigilant for His answers.

In my book *9 Days to Heaven: How to Make Everlasting Meaning of Your Life* there is a chapter headed: **Identifying God's guiding hand in your life**.

Here is an extract which I hope will help further.

God chooses many ways to contact us. When you pray for guidance of some sort it is important to be aware that in addition to talking to you directly God may use some other means to make contact. Say, for instance, you have prayed about a major dilemma. You may then be guided by a strong urge to speak about it to someone you had not considered.

They may:

Supply the answer you were seeking.

Or:

Provide the key to the next step.

Or:

Give you some comfort or support through understanding and empathy, which encourages you to keep going until the answer appears.

You will also garner more ideas on getting God's guidance from **Taking notice of God** which you read earlier.

I am confident that, after practising this for a while – keeping alert, being completely open and anticipating His contact – you will be able to make your own list in your Spiritual Enrichment notebook of the ways He has guided you.

How do you know that the guidance is from God?

Beloved, let us love one another; for love is of God, and he who loves is born of God and knows God. He who does not love does not know God; for God is love.
1 John 4:7–9

There we have it: God is Love and His ways are loving. So when you are inspired from a spirit of love this is always from God through His Holy Spirit – whether you have specifically prayed for guidance or not.

This love can show itself in numerous ways. Below, I give a few instances to get the ball rolling on scenarios that will probably be familiar to you.

Perhaps this has happened to you:
When you have prayed for guidance on a decision and you then feel, with absolute clarity, that you are on the good and right path: That guidance is from God.

Or you may experience this:
When you feel encouraged to do something for someone – a stranger or colleague or loved one: That encouragement is from God.

Maybe you have felt this way:
When you are in trouble and you pray and all of a sudden you feel calm and comforted – though nothing has changed: That comfort is from God.

Consider this:

When you feel inspired to create something beautiful or useful to others: That inspiration is from God.

On the other hand, if you feel vindictive, bitter, vengeful, or any other hurtful desire or emotion – whether you have prayed for guidance or not – that is the work of the Devil, whom Jesus describes as the "father of all lies" (John 8:44).

Bear in mind too that, as your relationship with Christ deepens, you can expect the bond between you to be tested by negative feelings, which can come right out of the blue. Don't be surprised either, if that extends to your faith itself being tested.

If you ever feel overcome by negativity, which can take many forms, pray. Use the following prayer or one of your own.

Prayer for a switch to love

Dear Lord,

I am full of negativity, and, knowing this offends You, I apologize from my heart.

I also know I am not worthy but will You please fill me with Your grace and so transform my feelings into loving ones.

I ask this in the name of Jesus Christ our Lord. Amen.

I hope that you are beginning to be comfortable with speaking to God in an informal way – as to your loving Heavenly Father. You may like to write about this in your Spiritual Enrichment notebook.

Section Two Overview

- Recommitting yourself to Christ gives a fresh start to your relationship.

- Discovering new ways to communicate with God enriches faith.

- When you speak to Christ, listen expectantly for His reply – in any number of guises.

Section Three

Give Your Day a Good Beginning and End

Centre Your Whole Day on Christ

This could well be the most important section in the book, because, through it you can nurture your relationship with Christ by a simple, yet highly effective, choice to focus on Him.

Actually, it was Christ Who highlighted this significance for me. And, mulling that over, I remembered that in my talks and workshops I meet many people who do not speak to God at the start of the day. Similarly, though they commonly *do* talk to God at night, their prayers are often garbled through fatigue.

If you recognize that pattern as yours, do not feel bad! Instead, know that you have just identified a wonderful opportunity to take a HUGE stride forward on your new spiritual journey. Choosing to build your day on the foundation of prayer will give everything deeper meaning. And it will give that confidence boost and add the lightness and brightness I mentioned in the **Preface**.

❖ **Found a gap in your prayer life? Fill it with Christ!**

Please don't panic now by thinking that this won't work for you as you definitely don't have any spare time, neither in the morning nor the evening, to do more praying! Bear with me and I will show you how time is not an issue; it never was. You will see that involving Christ in your day is more about deliberately choosing to think about Him rather than memorizing new prayers.

❖ **Even a quick word with God keeps Him involved in your life**

Yes, the list of prayers in this section *is* quite long but these are only suggestions which will, hopefully, trigger your own prayers relevant to you at the time. So when you have read through my selection – the ones I regularly use myself – choose what fits with your circumstances and add your own spin.

When you become familiar with this new method, you will be chatting away to Jesus without a thought about "lack of time". The richness this will bring to your everyday routine may amaze you!

❖ Even a short chat with Jesus can lift your spirits

Remember to record your growing happiness in your Spiritual Enrichment notebook.

You may find it a good idea to jot down dates, and perhaps say a little about what is happening in your life at the time. It could make for very interesting reading as the years go by.

And when you begin to talk to God from your heart, you could note how you feel about this and how your relationship is growing. This is something that we take a closer look at later.

Prayers upon waking

Begin to build the foundation of each new day by embracing the day as a gift, and thanking God for it.

You may wonder why you need to be grateful for every day but it is easy to forget that we are God's creation and our life depends completely upon Him. Our lungs are filled with air and our heart continues to beat – to name but two of our essential bodily processes – through God's generosity. And it is very grounding to remember that daily.

Many years ago, having read of people who, after a near-death experience, found a new appreciation of life, I decided to follow their example of appreciation – thankfully without the trauma.

That began by expressing gratitude, first of all, for waking up, and you may like to try this too. Begin by opening your eyes and then rubbing your fingertips together. Follow this with your first prayer of the day.

Prayer of thankfulness

Hello Lord.
Thank You for the gift of a new day. And thank You too that I can see and hear and touch, and for my other senses.
Please help me to use this day wisely.
I ask this in Jesus' name.
Amen.

If, perhaps, you had a restless night, or felt ill, or worried about something, you may like to add thanks that you feel better, or have come through the night unscathed. Whatever kind of night you had: give God the thanks for bringing you through it.

This is the day which the LORD has made; let us rejoice and be glad in it.
Psalm 118:24

Expressing thankfulness to God with a big smile on your face is, therefore, the perfect start to your day!

Morning Prayers

The time you can spare for a morning talk with God may well vary. Do remember too that the list of prayers below are only suggestions to set you on the right track. Each one is so short that it only takes a few seconds to say. And you could, for instance, say some of them on the move.

A wonderful way to start each day is by admiring God's creations in nature. I like to say my morning prayers, while the kettle is on for tea, looking out of the open back door after listening for a few moments to some pretty birdsong.

If you can't do that you could look out of the window at the sky. Or look at a houseplant or a cut flower. Or close your eyes and imagine you are walking on freshly mown grass, or beside the sea with a warm tangy breeze on your face.

No matter where you are, or how you feel, you can go anywhere you want to through your imagination!

Prayer of praise and thanks

Oh Lord,

You are so very wonderful! And for all your creations I give You praise.

Thank You so much for the gift of imagination. It is almost miraculous to be able to "go" wherever I want to and "see" whatever I want to with my mind's eye.

After praising and thanking your Creator, it is a good idea to ask for His help and guidance during your day. That way you can do what He wants you to – remembering you are playing your own special role in His great Plan. (More about this later.)

Prayer for guidance throughout the day

Dear Lord,

Please guide me today that I might do Your will, and that I may grow in love for myself, for others, and for You.

I ask this in the name of Jesus Christ our Lord. Amen.

As we are here on earth to be tested, in any day you could be called upon to face strong challenges. So, you may like to be prepared for these.

Prayer for courage

Oh Lord,

If I face any difficulties today, will You please remind me that You are always there at my side.

I ask this in Jesus' name. Amen.

You may well want to say a few prayers for your loved ones. Perhaps the following will help you frame your own requests.

Prayer for the protection of loved ones

Dear Lord,

Please look after: [name your family, friends and colleagues].

Please hold them, their families and friends, in the palm of Your hand, see them through their testing times, and bring them ever closer to You.

I ask this in the name of Jesus Christ our Lord. Amen.

I like to use this time to pray for my loved ones who have gone before me. Perhaps you would like to do that too.

Prayer for departed loved ones

Dear Lord,

For all my family, friends, and ancestors who have gone

before me, and especially [list your deceased family and friends], and for everyone who passed over yesterday, this morning, and who is passing over now, I ask that You invite them into Your heavenly kingdom for all eternity.

I ask this in Jesus' name. Amen.

If you have recently, or not so recently, lost a loved one and are grieving for them, talk to God – He understands and will see you through.

Prayer for the grieving

Dear Lord Jesus,

You said, "Blessed are those who mourn, for they shall be comforted" (Matthew 5:4).

Please let me feel Your comforting nearness today as I mourn the loss of my loved one.

I ask this through the same Christ our Lord. Amen.

If you have something difficult to do today, asking God's help ensures the best start and is the best way forward.

Prayer for help with a difficult day

Dear Lord,

You know that I am worried about what this day will bring so will You please fill me with Your Grace and love to help me through.

I ask this in the name of Jesus Christ our Lord. Amen.

Saying any of the above prayers, or any of your own, will firmly fix your mind on God as your centre – without being time consuming. I think you will quickly reap the benefit of this new mindset.

At the day's end

At the end of the day, in the pursuit of spiritual development, you may want to mull things over. You could spend a few precious moments with God, say, after you have eaten a meal and before you start to relax and unwind. Embrace this with joy and you will find that even one minute of His company will be a delightful part of your leisure.

As a review, you could ask yourself, for instance, if there were moments when you were not loving. Perhaps you were very busy and impatience spilled over into irritable words or actions. Or maybe you let someone down. Whatever comes to mind in your personal circumstances, if you discover something you could have done better, speak to God about it. Here are a few prayers to get you started.

Prayer for forgiveness

Dear Lord,

I am so sorry that I was not loving at all times today. I regret it. I ask for Your forgiveness. Please help and guide me tomorrow to avoid the same mistakes.

I ask this in the name of Jesus Christ our Lord. Amen.

If you have hurt someone's feelings, you could add this.

Prayer for the courage to apologize

Oh, Lord,

You know that I have hurt someone today. Please give me the courage to apologize to them.

I ask this in Jesus' name. Amen.

Maybe you were overcome by procrastination and squandered time instead of using it wisely. In that case you might like to speak to God about that.

Prayer to overcome procrastination

Dear Lord,

I am sorry that I did not use my time wisely today. I regret it. Will You please help and guide me tomorrow to make better use of both the time and the talents You have blessed me with.

I ask this in the name of Jesus Christ our Lord. Amen.

From the above few short prayers, I am sure that you get the idea. Whatever is applicable to your personal day, bring it before God. As I said at the start, you could do so in one minute if needs be. Yet that short time could be a loving and beautiful and powerful interlude with Christ!

Before you go to sleep

In a way, the end of a day is a sort of full-circle. As you expressed gratitude to God for the very fact that you woke up this morning, now is the time to thank Him for all the blessings of the day. If you are reeling from a very tough day and scrabbling to pinpoint those, go back to basics: food, shelter, loved ones, and so on.

Also, it is possible that you may go to sleep and not wake up again. Gosh! You may well not thank me for pointing that out. But. I don't regard that as morbid. As Christians, we are not of this world; this is *not* all there is. Remembering that you are God's creation and that one day – sooner or later – you will return back to your heavenly home keeps you walking along the right path.

Bearing this in mind, last thing at night, I always finish my prayers with this short and to the point prayer my mother taught me when I was a child. (The earliest version was by Joseph Addison.)

Prayer: Now I Lay Me Down to Sleep
Now I lay me down to sleep
I pray You Lord my soul to keep,
And if I die before I wake,
I pray You Lord my soul to take.

I next think of my family and friends and bring them before God. Perhaps you would like to do that too.

Prayer at night for loved ones
Dear Lord,
Please bless [name your closest loved ones] and all my family and friends. Please bring them safely through the night.
I ask this in Jesus' name. Amen.

In conclusion, I like to tell God what He means to me. You may like to do the same.

Prayer of praise, thanks and love

Oh Lord,
I praise You – Father, Son and Holy Spirit.
I thank You for the blessings of the day.
I love You God, my Heavenly Father.
I love You Jesus, my Saviour.
I love You Holy Spirit, You give me life and teach me.

If you find yourself lying awake with a mind buzzing with problems or dilemmas, why not ask God to take hold of them for a while?

Prayer to lay down your burdens

Dear Lord,
You know that I have some problems and we both know that at this very moment I can do nothing about any of them! So, will You please take the burden of them onto Your shoulders tonight so that I can sleep. Also, will You please guide me to a solution to my dilemmas tomorrow, or very soon.
I ask this in the name of Your Son, Jesus Christ. Amen.

By saying any of the above prayers, or any of your own, you will bring your day to a God-centred close. It could not be a more perfect completion of this day's spiritual journey.

Section Three Overview

- Show your gratitude to God for the gift of each day by talking to Him when you wake up.

- Involving Christ in planning your daily schedule deepens

your relationship.

- Reviewing each day with Christ's input keeps your focus on His ways.

- Thanking God for all blessings is the perfect ending to the day.

Section Four

Christianity as a Lifestyle

Love Thy Neighbour

There can be little doubt that taking our faith out into the world can be tricky at times. You never know who or what you are going to meet along the way, and what tests may arise.

In this section we take a look at a selection of situations that you may well find yourself in on an average day. How you act or react is one aspect of every test. In this book though, our focus is on prayer. As you journey through the following scenarios let the prayers be a catalyst to your own prayers relating to the many other experiences which may crop up in your life.

❖ **Take every opportunity to pray for others**

Jesus told us that we should love everyone, not just those we pick and choose and feel closest to.

> *You shall love your neighbour as yourself.*
> **Mark 12:31**

As Christians we are therefore encouraged to be as loving and considerate as possible. It is good to remember that you are an ambassador for Christ, and to try to let that shine through as often as you humanly can. Try the following prayer to ask His help with that.

Prayer to be loving
Dear Lord Jesus,
Please help me to be as loving as possible to each and every person I meet and interact with.
And in doing so may people recognize You in me.
I ask this in Your name Lord. Amen.

Keeping this in mind, and without anyone knowing, you can diligently pray for those around you – be they acquaintances, or strangers. They could be in need, or simply going about their business, but everyone can benefit from your prayers (as you can from theirs).

❖ **Ask God to bless everyone around you**

Prayer for a stranger

Dear Lord,
Please give that person everything they are dreaming of and more, and bring them ever closer to You.
I ask this in the name of Jesus Christ our Lord. Amen.

The role of the clergy in representing Christ on earth cannot be overestimated. These people dedicate their lives to God. They teach us His ways and support and encourage us in our faith so you may like to remember their tireless work in your prayers.

Prayer for the clergy

Dear Lord,
Please watch over, bless, strengthen, protect, and inspire those whom You have called to minister to our souls. Keep them strong in faith in a shifting world that needs, more than ever, their example of holiness.
I ask this in Jesus' name. Amen.

At any time in our life, we may need medical help of some sort. What would we do without those who spend their lives trying to help others in caring for the sick and/or vulnerable? So you may like to remember them in your prayers.

Prayer for health care staff

Dear Lord,

Please watch over, bless, strengthen and protect doctors and nurses, and all other staff working with the sick and/or vulnerable such as in hospitals, or private practices.

I ask this in the name of Jesus Christ Your Son. Amen.

To keep society running smoothly we rely on a lot of help from a variety of sources. Some may be considered more important than others but each role, in its way, forms an essential part of a community so you may like to remember the people involved in your prayers.

Prayer for those providing essential services

Dear Lord,

Please bless and watch over all those whose work and services we rely on. These include: carers, teachers and their aides, supermarket staff, plumbers, electricians, post office workers, refuse collectors, delivery drivers, and so on.

I ask this in Jesus' name. Amen.

When I look at a newspaper, or read on the web, or hear on the radio or television that someone has died, I pray. There are other versions of the following prayer but this is the one I always use.

Prayer for the dead: The Eternal Rest Prayer

Eternal rest give unto them O Lord, and let perpetual light shine upon them.

May they rest in peace.

Amen.

I hope that the above gives you food for thought, so that, as you go about your busy daily life, you frequently remember others and their struggles and include them in your prayers.

You may like to keep notes about your new ideas for prayers in your Spiritual Enrichment book.

Pray before eating

Praying before eating is a ritual that you may or may not have adopted. Often it will depend on your upbringing. But even if you don't usually say Grace before meals, you can always choose again.

There are many reasons to pray before eating. The top one for me is gratitude that I have food to eat. Because not everyone is blessed with enough food. In some countries the difference between food on the table or not depends on whether or not, for instance, rain falls on that season's crops.

Have you ever considered that every morsel of food you have ever eaten has been provided by God? Without the seed, rain, sunshine, bees, and so on that He gives none of us would have food to eat.

For years I have prayed before I eat. I wasn't always so scrupulous about this but a stranger set me a good example and kick-started the habit. The life-change happened one day on a plane.

Before eating lunch, the man sitting beside me made the Sign of the Cross. This told me a few things about him. First, that he was a Christian. Second, that he was thankful to God for his food. And third, that he was happy to show his thanks and faith to the world.

I mulled that over and made myself a promise to follow his good example – whether alone or with company, at home or out and about. And I have stuck to that. To the well-known prayers, I add a little extra.

Prayer of gratitude for food

Dear Lord,
Thank You for blessing me with the gift of this nourishing food. I know that without You nothing would grow. In gratitude, as I eat, I will savour each mouthful.

Before moving on, hold that thought of gratitude for a few moments. Just a gentle reminder: even a small donation to a charity which helps to feed the hungry will help. Perhaps you have a favourite organization. These two are mine:

CAFOD is an international development charity and the official aid agency of the Catholic Church in England and Wales. They reach out to people living in poverty with practical help, whatever their religion or culture. See: https://cafod.org.uk

Mary's Meals provides life-changing meals to some of the world's poorest children every day they attend school. See: https://www.marysmeals.org.uk

No matter how much or how little you can afford to give to your personal favourite organizations, try to remember to keep them and those they help in your prayers.

Drive as a Christian

Here I use driving as an example of an everyday activity where we can interact with others in a loving way. Hopefully, it will prompt you to think up other prayers in the variety of situations you regularly find yourself.

I really enjoy driving my car but I am aware that it can be dangerous out there on the roads. So before I drive, I like to say a quick prayer.

Prayer for safety when driving
Bear us up on eagles' wings dear Heavenly Father.
I ask this in the name of Jesus Christ our Lord. Amen.

Out on the road you can meet with any number of situations. You may find the following prayers help you to cope.

Prayers for use before and during driving
Dear Lord,
Please help me to drive safely today.
I ask this in Jesus' name. Amen.

Dear Lord,
Please help me to remain courteous to my fellow drivers at all times.
I ask this in Jesus' name. Amen.

Dear Heavenly Father,
Please keep me alert to the changing speed limits, and so on, along the roads, especially the quirky changes which can be so very dangerous.
I ask this in Jesus' name. Amen.

Oh Lord,

The driver of the car behind me is pushing me to break the speed limit. In this built-up area that would be dangerous as well as illegal. Please help us both to keep calm, stay within the law, and keep safe.

I ask this in Jesus' name. Amen.

My heart goes out to all the dead birds, hedgehogs, foxes, and so on that I see on or beside the road. They were often crossing to get some food and had been hit by a vehicle. Instead of merely feeling sad, I take it a step further and say a little prayer of compassion.

Prayer for dead creatures

Dear Lord,

Please bring this poor dead creature to You and love them.

I ask this in the name of Jesus Christ our Lord. Amen.

Quite often, out driving, you can come across emergency services helping those in trouble. Picture yourself driving along in heavy traffic when, in your rear-view mirror, you see the flashing blue light of an ambulance and hear its siren wailing. After you pull over or make way to let it pass, what do you do next?

As a child, some friends used to say the rhyme that went: "Touch fingers, touch toes, never go in one of those." But after joining in a few times it just didn't seem the right thing to be saying or doing. After all, someone was in trouble. I decided to say a prayer for them instead. I still do this.

I also say the same prayer when I see or hear any other emergency vehicle such as a paramedic car, a police car, or a fire engine.

Prayer for an emergency situation

Dear Lord,

Please bring Your love, Your mercy, Your consolation, Your help, and Your healing to those involved in this emergency situation, and in every emergency situation happening throughout the world now.

I ask this in the name of Jesus Christ our Lord. Amen.

Perhaps the above has broadened your thinking on how much your actions and decisions can affect the lives of others. Being loving, and therefore considerate and prayerful, can truly benefit everyone – including you!

Bring God into your daily work

No matter what your age and situation, your day will usually be filled with tasks. Some may be mundane, others challenging, and, who knows they could even be very rewarding. Irrespective of your personal role in life, the most important thing for the practice of your Christian faith is to try to do everything with love. In this way, as you work, God's Spirit can work in you. Then, even the most menial task can be an opportunity for spiritual growth.

Before I start work of any sort, especially my writing, I ask God to come and be my partner to help and guide me, and show me what He wants me to do. You may like to try this for yourself.

Prayer for guidance with work

Dear Lord,

Please come and partner with me in this task and help me to work with love. [You may like to add in some specifics now.] Also, will You please guide me so that I do what You want me to.

I ask this in the name of Jesus Christ our Lord. Amen.

Sometimes, you may come up against a task that, no matter how big an effort you make, it won't come right. If you have been beavering away at something but getting nowhere fast, take a look at the following:

Unless the LORD builds the house,
those who build it labour in vain.
Unless the LORD watches over the city,
the watchman stays awake in vain.
It is in vain that you rise up early and go to bed late to rest,
eating the bread of anxious toil;

for he gives to his beloved sleep.
Psalm 127:1–2

Is that striking any chords with you? If you identify with those words, you may find the following 4-step meditation helpful.

Meditation

Step 1.
Take a deep breath. Breathe out slowly and relax.

Step 2.
Now, look at the Psalm verses again. Read them over very slowly. If you are alone, read them aloud.

Step 3.
Close your eyes and let that sink deep into your spirit for a few moments.

Now say this prayer.

Prayer for forgiveness and guidance

Dear Lord,
I am so sorry that I have tried to work without Your guidance. I did not think to ask for Your thoughts and comments. It is now plain to me why this task has been so difficult. Thank You for this revelation. Please will You show me what You want me to do with it now.

I ask this in Jesus' name. Amen.

Step 4.
Listen now for a few moments to anything the Lord may want to tell you. As you carry on with your task, be vigilant for His guidance.

Tackling any work in a spirit of love will lighten the load.

When working with others this can have a beneficial effect on everyone. When someone is out to do their best it is a wonderful influence. Conversely, people who are resentful and moody pollute the atmosphere and add pressure.

Whatever form your daily work takes – either at home or out in the world – I hope that the above helps you to be creative in bringing the love of God into every twist and turn and interaction.

You are on earth for a reason

When we are born, and begin to grow, we usually do not know why we are on earth. God made us, though, so that we would, to paraphrase Acts 17:27, feel about a bit and in doing so find Him. And you have found Him, which is the most important thing in your life!

The nearer you draw to Christ, though, the more you may feel the thirst to know what He sent you to earth to do. Because there *is* something that only you can do.

Try the following 3-step meditation to become even more open to God's will and His path for your life.

Meditation

Step 1.
Take a deep breath. Breathe out slowly and relax.

Step 2.
Read over this prayer.

> ### Prayer to discover your personal role in God's Plan
> Dear Lord,
> I want to do Your will. So please will You show me what it is that You want of me.
> I ask this in Jesus's name. Amen.

Step 3.
Spend a few moments in God's loving presence and listen for anything He may want to tell you now. As you go about your daily life, keep open to any guidance God gives.

Consider this: by keeping alert for God's guidance, you will be carrying out His will!

Begin to think of ways that you can use your God-given talents to help others. Maybe to encourage, bring joy, express empathy, bring food; the possibilities are endless.

Often a clue to your special role can be indicated through, say, a cause which prompts passionate concern, or even anger. You may rail, "*They* should do something about that!"

If such a pressing scenario occurs to you, ask God to show you what YOU can do about it. Prayer is the best starting point.

You have been drawing closer to God by speaking to Him in a new way and, hopefully, it has already sweetened your life. This is because when you invite God to participate fully in your day-to-day living you can be sure that with His help and guidance you will have more confidence (as previously mentioned), and greater clarity and purpose.

Life is more satisfying, and far less confusing, when we let Jesus help us to do what *He* wants of us more often.

Don't forget to keep a track of that in your Spiritual Enrichment notebook. I hope that by now your insights are building up.

Even the briefest Thank You to God has value

I like to say Thank You to God a lot, often in a very quick and simple way. Perhaps you may like to say one, a few, or all of the following prayers.

Prayers of thanksgiving

Dear Lord, thank You for the gift of each new day.

Dear Lord, I thank You for the gift of faith.

Dear Lord, thank You for the gift of a loving family.

Dear Lord, I thank You for the gift of loving friends.

Dear Lord, I thank You for the gift of being loved.

Dear Lord, thank You for the gift of being able to love.

Dear Lord, I thank You for the gift of good health.

Dear Lord, I thank You for gifting me with an appreciation of nature.

Dear Lord, I thank You for gifting me with an appreciation of all kinds of music.

Dear Lord, I thank You for the gift of my love of animals.

I am certain that you can add many personal thanks to this list – which barely scratches the surface of all that I am thankful for in my life. While your heart is open and focussed, you may like to jot down in your Spiritual Enrichment notebook some of your own reasons for thankfulness.

Also, as I mentioned at the start of the Section, it only contains some examples of the kind of prayers that may be relevant to your life. I feel sure that you have begun to think of many other people, or groups of people, whom you would like to pray for on a regular basis. You could record these too in your notebook.

Section Four Overview

- Let your prayers be inclusive.

- Live out your Christian faith in all you do.

- Find your purpose in life by asking God what He wants of you.

Section Five

When Life Gets Challenging

The prayers below can be said at any time, and in any place. However, when you have a little more time you could also use them with the 5-step method outlined in Section Two under the heading: **Asking God for help and guidance**.

Take Your Troubles to Your Heavenly Father

The path of life is not always smooth. In this section we look at a selection of issues that may crop up along the way. Perhaps some will apply to you. Maybe none of the details will fit perfectly. But the method can be adapted to address most of your troubles.

No matter what the issue is though, turn to God for help. It could be that He will not take the trouble away but His presence will see you through.

❖ Whatever the problem, share it with God

It is a good idea to begin by asking God for a new way to look at the challenges you are facing. Try the following prayer to get you started and bring love into the equation.

Prayer for a new outlook

Oh Lord,
You know everything about me and the reasons for everything happening in my life right now. Please help me to see the lesson in my situation. Show me how I can grow in love through these tests.
I ask this in Jesus' name. Amen.

Try saying the above prayer, or one of your own, a few times throughout the day. You could say it when you are in your car stuck in traffic, or in a queue at the supermarket, or on a bus, or wherever. God can speak to you anywhere, and at any time.

❖ Listen expectantly for God's communications

Before we look at specifics, let's cover an overarching occurrence in life. No matter how strong you are, or how deep your faith, it is all too easy to feel temporarily overwhelmed. You don't need to be in a bad place in your life for this to sweep over you. It can occur just as easily when things are generally good but, for instance, a number of minor, but trying things, accumulate, or you are extremely busy and small tasks stack up.

If you identify this swamping of spirit, speak to God about it immediately. Try the following 3-step meditation to regain perspective and to move forward.

Meditation

Step 1.
Take a deep breath. Breathe out slowly and relax.

Step 2.
Read over this prayer.

Prayer for when you feel overwhelmed
Dear Lord,
I am beginning to feel overwhelmed, so will You please help me to calm down so I can see the situation more clearly. Then, will You please show me if there is anything I can do to move forward, perhaps by prioritizing, and taking even one small step to deal with any aspect at all.
I ask this in Jesus' name. Amen.

Step 3.
Spend a few moments in God's loving presence and listen attentively for anything He may want to tell you now. As you carry on with your day keep alert for any guidance God may want to give you.

When you follow God's guidance, and take some form of action to begin to alleviate your situation, it is highly likely that you will feel great relief. That may well be enough to regain your equilibrium. If it isn't, try saying the above prayer again to help you with the next step, and so on.

If you feel despair

It is not uncommon, at times, to be so overcome by life and circumstances that you feel despair. In the Bible there are a number of instances where even the most holy of people temporarily felt like giving up. The prophet Elijah was but one of these – as you can read in 1 Kings, chapter 19, verses 1 to 8.

Elijah journeyed into the wilderness, then sat down under a broom tree and asked that he might die.

It is enough; now, O LORD, take away my life...
1 Kings 19:4

Happily, God did not take Elijah's life! Instead, He strengthened him to continue with his mission.

If *you* ever feel desperate, please understand that despair is of the Devil: the father of all lies, at work again. This time he is telling you the nonsense that you are alone and it is all too much.

The reality is: THE HOLY SPIRIT IS WITH YOU AND HIS STRENGTH WILL BRING YOU THROUGH THIS TEST.

Grasp onto this fact as a lifeline.

Say the following prayer aloud, as many times as you need to.

Prayer for rekindling of hope
Heavenly Father,

Please help me.

Please keep me safe in Your loving hands until I feel strong again.

I beg this in Jesus' name. Amen.

Keep in mind God's love for you. Remember that, though all of life is a test, Jesus Christ, Who knows first-hand about great suffering, will not let you fall!

When you feel better you might like to write up your experiences in your Spiritual Enrichment notebook. Putting together the facts and the good outcome may also make it easier for you to share these methods where they can be of help and assistance to another.

Talk to God when you are angry

In the midst of anger, which can be deeply upsetting to the spirit, *prayer* may be the last thing on your mind. Maybe then, it is the ideal time to talk things over with God.

There are many reasons why we get angry. It is human to feel this emotion, which can arise in numerous situations. Here though, we take a look at just two types of anger to get you thinking. The first type is the anger that you would prefer not to feel – so let's call it Avoidable Anger. The second type is the anger which may be a catalyst for doing good – so let's call it Justifiable Anger.

Avoidable Anger is often caused by an escalation of irritation. Try the following 4-step meditation to gain an insight into the way you usually handle this.

Meditation

Step 1.

Take a deep breath. Breathe out slowly and relax. Sit for a few moments and ask Christ to help you to learn something about yourself.

Step 2.

Now, think about the last time you were angry when it could have been avoided. Perhaps you felt upset by the thoughtlessness of a loved one, or even a stranger. Or, whatever... The permutations are endless.

Step 3.

Did your anger only fuel the situation? In hindsight, do you wish you had kept your cool? If the answer is Yes to either question, this prayer may help to diffuse things next time.

Prayer for a peaceful heart and loving mind

Oh, Lord,

I am sorry that I feel so angry. You know why I am upset but please help me to calm down.

And please flood the person I am angry at with Your gracious love.

I humbly ask this in Jesus' name. Amen.

Step 4.

Listen for a few moments for anything Christ has to say to you.

Justifiable Anger is the one that you feel is absolutely warranted. Try the following 4-step meditation to gain an insight into the way you usually handle this.

Meditation

Step 1.

Take a deep breath. Breathe out slowly and relax. Sit for a few moments and ask Christ to help you to learn something about yourself.

Step 2.

Now, think about the last time you were justifiably angry. Perhaps, for instance, you witnessed or heard of some form of cruelty. Was there anything you could have done to prevent that happening? Or to mitigate the situation? Did you seek God's guidance at the time?

Step 3.

If you are still angry about whatever happened, talk it over with God. For the future, in the face of evil behaviour in anyone, quickly take the matter to the Lord in prayer.

Prayer to neutralize evil

Dear Lord Jesus,

I beg You to flood [this person/these people/this organization] with Your merciful love so that it kick-starts the consciences of those involved and turns them away from evil deeds.

I ask this through the same Christ our Lord. Amen.

Step 4.

Listen for a few moments for anything Christ has to say to you.

You may like to record any insights from these two meditations in your Spiritual Enrichment notebook. If you get any more communications about this from Christ, you could add those too.

When you find some people irritating

Sometimes our personalities clash with others' and it seems that no matter how hard we try, we do not feel comfortable in their company. But as Christians, we are obligated to be on good terms with everyone.

If possible, so far as it depends upon you, live peaceably with all.
Romans 12:18

Try to remind yourself that this clash is a test. As with every other test, love is the answer and God is the One to help us tap into that.

Prayer for peace in all your relationships
Dear Lord Jesus,
Please help me to walk a peaceful and loving path with everyone I come into contact with in my life.
I ask this through the same Christ our Lord. Amen.

In an especially difficult situation, try to turn things around by asking God's blessings on the person with whom you are upset.

Prayer for blessings on those you don't get along with
Oh, Lord,
You know those whom I dislike, though I am trying hard to feel loving towards them.
Please shower them with Your Divine love, give them everything they are dreaming of, and bring them ever closer to You.
I ask this in Jesus' name. Amen.

You have probably come across the theory that we cannot stand our own faults in others. That being the case, you could, as a prayerful spiritual development exercise, try to discover if that is at the root of your dislike for a particular person. If it is, you can then choose, for the love of God, to use this self-knowledge to eradicate your own fault.

Coping with sickness

When we are ill, life can be very difficult. Not for nothing do people say that good health is vital, and without it we can do little. Health is therefore looked upon by many as a gift.

Often though, good health can be the product of a number of informed lifestyle choices.

Yet sometimes, we just do get ill – or even injured. And that, combined with the physical weakness frequently experienced as the body directs its focus to a cellular war (or repair), can bring on feelings of loneliness.

Fortunately, you do not have to endure the illness alone. You are in the company of Christ, and, no matter what, He will help you through everything. Simply remembering that fact can get you through the worst of it. So as soon as you are able, speak to Him and ask for His help. Try the following prayer, or one of your own.

Prayer for recovery

Oh Lord,
Please hold me in the palm of Your hand and see me through this testing time.
And Lord, please heal me from my illness (or injury).
I ask this in Jesus' name. Amen.

Watching a loved one going through an illness can be very upsetting. I have heard, for instance, many parents say that they would gladly suffer the illness instead of watching their child go through it. There can be such a strong and almost overwhelming feeling of helplessness at times like these, even when you trust the doctors and nurses and their treatments.

But actually, no matter if it is a child or an adult who is sick (or injured), there is *always* something you can do to help.

You can turn to God and ask for His healing. Try the following prayer, or one of your own.

Prayer for the recovery of a loved one

Oh Lord,

Please hold [name the person] in the palm of Your hand and see them through this testing time. And Lord, please heal them from their illness (or injury).

I ask this in Jesus' name. Amen.

In the case of serious illness (or injury), affecting either you or a loved one, it is a good idea to involve others by asking them to pray too for recovery. As Jesus taught us: praying together for a single cause is a very powerful thing to do.

> *Again I say to you, if two of you agree on earth about anything they ask, it will be done for them by my Father in heaven.*
> **Matthew 18:19**

I have witnessed many healings through using this method. The pattern I have seen is that the problem that was diagnosed by medical professionals as "major" turned out to be "minor" in the end. I am, of course, describing miracles.

Before leaving this topic, I want to add that serious illness or accidents, happening to ourselves or loved ones, often bring up the question: WHY? And the deeper the pain, the louder the question.

All I want to say is that, many years ago, after going through an extremely testing time related to a close relative, I eventually made the decision to put that question aside. I did so because, continuing to question, without receiving a satisfactory answer, was preventing me from getting the spiritual help I needed from Christ.

You know and *I* know that many things in this life are *un*knowable. That is where Faith comes in. So, to speak plainly: I don't know why bad things happen. But *I* decided to keep putting my trust in my loving Heavenly Father.

I hope that, if you are ever challenged in a very painful way, you can do that too. Though sometimes, that acceptance will come only after a period of shock, then struggle. May God continue to hold you in the palm of His hand as you work your way through the situation.

When you cannot forgive

When we feel hurt by someone in some way, it is human to resist forgiving them. But forgiveness is an essential part of Christian living.

> And forgive us our debts;
> *As we also have forgiven our debtors;*
> **Matthew 6:12**

Looking at the Bible quote above, you will surely recognize (though maybe worded slightly differently) this extract of the Lord's Prayer – which is a huge challenge that Christians try to rise to. When you say it, you are asking God to deal with you as you deal with others. Wow. That's a sobering thought, is it not?

But Christ's words here –and at many other times – go far beyond their face value. For one thing, consider the fact that our pain and disappointment often increases if we allow it to fester in our mind. But, if you forgive that won't happen, so forgiveness, of itself, will be of benefit. And then, consider too, that the only person feeling your pain is you! That begs the question: Why are you continuing to hurt yourself?

This is such a common situation. Many people find it so very difficult to forgive. You probably know someone who has allowed a painful episode to sour the rest of their life. Their bitterness and negativity often infects the lives of those around them too. You would probably agree that that is a waste of the possibility of a joyful life!

But, to put the focus back onto you: it is possible that right now you are feeling angry with... *me*. You could be thinking something like: If she only knew what they had done to me, she wouldn't dare be writing this!

So let me say straight out that I am sorry for your pain. Very.

However, I do not want you to suffer anymore because you will not forgive the sin against you – grievous though it clearly was.

I do urge you now to choose to set yourself free through forgiveness – which in no way condones what someone has done. Try the following 3-step meditation to reinforce your decision.

Meditation

Step 1.
Take a deep breath. Breathe out slowly and relax.

Step 2.
Take a few moments to think about your choice to be forgiving.

Step 3.
Say the following prayer slowly and aloud if circumstances permit.

Prayer to set aside resistance to forgive

Oh, Lord,
You alone know the depth of my pain and so I beg You to please help me to forgive the person I blame for it. And in doing so, will You please let me feel the freedom which comes from doing Your will?
I ask this in the name of Your blessed Son, our Lord Jesus Christ. Amen.

Very deep hurt can take time to heal. And healing is a process. It may even take therapy. But forgiveness remains a crucial part of healing. I have witnessed people who, even after extensive therapy, refused to forgive, and so remain stuck in their pain. So I continue to urge you to choose to forgive.

In very difficult circumstances the first step towards forgiving could be a willingness to undertake it.

As you repeat the above prayer, or better still, your own

customized version – on a regular basis and in a heartfelt way – you are on the path towards complete healing. You may also find it helpful to use the method outlined in Section Two under the heading **Asking God for help and guidance** in order to reach your goal.

Before leaving this topic, I want to mention that the person you may need to forgive is YOU; yourself! If that is the case then you are possibly weighed down by Guilt. But, as we have identified, almost at the start of your new spiritual journey, you cannot change one jot of your past. And you have already told God in Section Two in the **Prayer for a fresh start** that you are sorry for anything that has offended Him and asked him to help you to forgive yourself, too, so that you were set free. So, I do urge you to, once and for all accept the reality of that, pray about it, and move on.

Try the following 5-step meditation to finally set yourself free to live a life of joy in Christ's company.

Meditation

Step 1.
Take a deep breath. Breathe out slowly and relax.

Step 2.
Take a few moments to think about the feelings of guilt (or anything else) which are blocking your peace of mind.

Step 3.
Ask yourself if there is any way to make amends for what created the feelings of guilt (or such like). Is there, for instance, someone you have hurt whom you could apologize to?

Step 4.
Say the following prayer, or one of your own.

Prayer to be set free of guilt

Dear Heavenly Father,

You alone know the feelings of guilt (or anything else) which stab at me and destroy my peace of mind. Firstly, I want to tell You that I am so very sorry for [tell God the specifics]. I want to make amends in any way possible, so please will You show me what You want me to do about this. And please will You help me to feel Your loving forgiveness.

I ask this in Jesus' name. Amen.

Step 5.

Listen for a few moments to anything your Heavenly Father wants to tell you now. As you go about your daily life, keep open for His guidance to free you from this debilitating issue.

As you have read through the prayers in this section, you may well have uncovered other troubles that you want to talk to your Heavenly Father about – maybe even on a regular basis. If that is the case you could record these in your Spiritual Enrichment notebook as a reminder.

You may also find it very useful to turn one or more of these personal prayers into a meditation using the one above as a guide. This will help to focus your conversation with God about a particular problem for added support and help.

Section Five Overview

• Sharing troubles with Christ brings relief.

• Mindfulness of the continual presence of the Holy Spirit gives added strength.

• Let asking for God's help become a habit.

Section Six

Let Biblical Inspiration Fire Your Imagination!

Slot Bible-Reading into Your Everyday Life

Although written thousands of years ago, the Bible, a collection of books, is as fresh and relevant today as it was then. Having read that sentence you may have difficulty accepting it, but bear with me. All will become clearer as you read this section and try out my technique for creating lively experiences from the ancient texts.

When you have tried this out it will, hopefully, encourage you to regular Bible reading. Unfortunately, even the most convinced of us can still allow reading the Word of God to get squeezed out of routine life. But, it is essential to find the time to do this so that we come to know more about God and His ways.

❖ **Get to know God better through His Word**

If you have never read the whole Bible – both Old and New Testaments – you are really missing out on invaluable insights into the Holy Trinity.

As you make your way through the passages, you surely *will* begin to marvel at how much content applies to your own life. Especially if, before you begin to read, you say a prayer like the following.

Prayer for help to relate to the Bible
Dear Lord,
As I read Your Word, will You please show me how it connects with my personal experiences.
I ask this in Jesus' name. Amen.

❖ **Let Christ show how your experiences relate to Him**

If you already regularly read the Bible, try saying the following prayer to renew the experience.

Prayer for new insights

Dear Heavenly Father,

As I read Your Word today please show me fresh insights into this familiar text.

I ask this in the name of Your Son, Jesus Christ. Amen.

When I read passages that are very familiar and then a new aspect springs out of it – which refreshes the text – I often get mesmerized by the new insight. I recommend adding your own insights to your Spiritual Enrichment notebook. It will make very interesting reading from time to time.

Bring the Bible alive

When you have a little time to spare – even ten minutes would do – bring the Bible stories alive by interacting with them through the amazing power of your imagination which we have already thanked God for.

As you go through each scenario, try to engage with your full creative potential. You could use the following list of questions to get the creative juices flowing.

Question 1.
What does the scenery looks like?

Maybe you see in your mind's eye that the terrain is flat, hilly, or even mountainous. Perhaps you imagine olive trees or other kinds of greenery. Maybe you see grey rocks or beige stretches of sand. Or you could see mainly buildings.

Question 2.
What are the characters wearing?

Maybe you see them in flowing robes. Perhaps you envisage the women in bright colours and the men more plainly dressed – or vice versa. You may picture some with head coverings.

Question 3
What is the weather like?

You could picture a hot and sunny day where your characters would benefit from shade. Or, you may see it as cold and grey and dismal, and imagine your characters shivering and blowing on their hands to warm them up.

Question 4.
What sounds can you hear around you?

Your imagination could conjure up birdsong, a dog barking,

or the braying of a donkey. Maybe you hear the call of a street vendor, or laughter from a group of friends. Perhaps from a nearby hill, you hear the tinkle of goat bells as a herd wanders and feeds.

Use these suggestions if they help, but don't get bogged down in the detail. As you begin to envisage the scenarios you will find the way that works best for you.

I have picked a few of my favourite Bible passages to help you to try this out. If you have never used this method, it will surely be a revelation. (The same method can be applied to other forms of worship or prayer to tease out hidden insights into what happened *then* and how it relates directly to you *now*.)

Zacchaeus the tax collector meets Jesus

Here we focus on the account written in the Gospel of Luke, chapter 19, verses 1 to 10. It is a favourite of mine because whenever I hear or read the passage, it always makes me smile with fondness for Zacchaeus.

I find him endearing because the short story shows a huge progression in his character under the influence of Christ. And I suspect that no one is more surprised by that than Zacchaeus himself.

In just a few paragraphs as we witness a life transformed, it gives me hope in a fallen world. It is a reminder that with God all things are possible so we can continue to trust in Him.

To help deepen the whole experience bear in mind the above 4 questions as you carry out the following 3-step visualization.

Visualization

Step 1.
Take a deep breath. Breathe out slowly and relax.

Step 2.
Say this prayer.

Prayer for understanding of Zacchaeus' conversion
Dear Lord Jesus,
Please help me bring to life the day You met Zacchaeus so I can learn more about the event and how it relates to me.
I ask this in Your name Lord and I thank You.

Step 3.
Embark on a journey of discovery by putting yourself into the shoes of Zacchaeus.

I am Zacchaeus, a chief tax collector in Jericho. Although rich and important, I do confess that I am not much liked. I know this is because I charge some people too much tax, but all the tax collectors do it so why shouldn't I make some extra money too? That's what I tell myself anyway.

I am on my way home from work. It is a warm sunny evening and I am looking forward to a good meal. But, wait a minute, there is a crowd of people coming towards me. They are very noisy. I hope it's not trouble.

Oh, they look happy and excited, so that's alright. Not a mob then. But more people are spilling out of houses along the roadside and joining up with the throng as they come towards me. I must say, I would really like to know what it's all about.

Right then. I've just asked someone and learned something extraordinary. The crowd has gathered around an important teacher named Jesus. He is said to have performed all sorts of miracles. He has cured many who were ill, and even raised the dead back to life! The people I asked were adamant that that had happened. Apparently there were many witnesses.

[See in your mind's eye the crowd swelling in number and sweeping towards you – though still a way off. Feel a great curiosity overcome you to see this man Jesus.]

I want to see the teacher. But at this rate, with so very many people surrounding Him, I won't be able to. This is because I am not tall, in fact, I am very short. What will I do? I feel agitated.

Something inside me is stirred up. It's like I just *have* to look upon this man with my own eyes. I feel compelled to do it. I glance up at the sky for inspiration then notice a nearby sycamore tree.

Hmm. I haven't climbed a tree since I was a boy. But the crowd is getting nearer so with no more hesitation I grasp hold of the lowest branch and heave myself upwards. Right then, if I part some branches I will surely be able to see the teacher as He passes beneath me.

I am breathing heavily after the exertion and I wipe my forehead with a handkerchief. I must say I'm glad no one can see me. It wouldn't do much for my reputation.

Oh, here He comes.

Oh, my goodness. He has stopped right under my tree!

"Zacchaeus, come down," Jesus says.

What? We have never met so how does the teacher know my name? But I don't have time to think it through as He is telling me that He wants to come to my house.

The crowd is laughing as I clamber down to the ground but I don't care. I feel that the teacher is doing me a great honour and I am filled with joy. I dare to look into Jesus' eyes. He smiles at me as if He really likes me. I feel like I am floating on air.

Then I "fall" back down again. I know I have done nothing to deserve this preferential treatment. But we are walking along towards my home and the teacher is so friendly that He puts me at ease.

My wife quickly organizes the servants to prepare the dining room and soon the best food is being brought in on platters and a cordial time is had by all. But then I hear someone saying, quite loudly, something nasty about Jesus eating with sinners. The teacher and I look at each other knowingly. He doesn't speak.

[Imagine yourself in the presence of Jesus with His eyes knowing all your sins.]

I look down at my hands. My heart is pounding. I can't explain it but I feel a changed man. I look up again at the teacher. He smiles at me. I take a deep breath and stand up.

I say to Him, loud enough for all present to hear, "I am going to give half of all I own to the poor. And I will pay back those I have cheated by four times the amount." When I say those words, I feel a huge weight – which I did not know I was carrying – lift off my shoulders. It was the right thing to do.

Jesus looks at me and smiles. Then He looks around. "Today salvation has come to this house," He tells the people. "Because this man too is a son of Abraham and the Son of man has come to seek out and save the lost."

I shiver at His words. I had not felt that I was a bad man, well, not bad enough to be "lost", damned, anyway. But now I know different. Then though, I feel that incredible lightness fill me again. Jesus has said that I am saved. What started out as an ordinary day has turned into the best, the most important day, of my life!

[Take this opportunity now to tell God all that is weighing down your conscience. Everything. Then tell Him how sorry you are and promise not to repeat these sins. Feel that incredible lightness which Zacchaeus experienced fill your whole being as you realize that you too are saved through accepting Jesus as your Saviour.]

[Ask Jesus if there is anything He especially wants to tell you now.]

The man born blind

Here we focus on the account written in the Gospel of John, chapter 9, verses 1 to 41. This is a passage that always makes me smile. The wisdom of the uneducated man, born blind then given sight by Christ, is striking. The way he shows up the determinedly closed minds of the Pharisees highlights the saying that goes, "There are none so blind as those who will not see."

And this is as prevalent today as 2,000+ years ago, which the passage reminds me of.

To help deepen the whole experience, bear in mind the way you brought the last scenario to life as you carry out the following 3-step visualization.

Visualization

Step 1.
Take a deep breath. Breathe out slowly and relax.

Step 2.
Say this prayer.

Prayer for understanding of the significance of the man's cure

Dear Lord Jesus,
Please will You help me to relive the day that You cured the man born blind. And please show me too how that relates to my own life.
I ask this in Your name Lord and I thank You.

Step 3.
Embark on a journey of discovery by putting yourself into the place of the man born blind.

I am sitting, as I do each day, outside the temple door. It is very hot and I am thankful to be in the shade. Then I hear some people approaching and hope they will drop a few coins into my begging bowl. But instead someone says, "Rabbi, who sinned, this man or his parents that he was born blind?"

Well, blind I may be but deaf I am not! But before I can say something cutting, the rabbi, apparently called Jesus, says, "Neither he nor his parents sinned, he was born blind so that the works of God may be revealed in him."

Well, I don't know what He means by that but seconds later He is rubbing something wet and sticky onto my eyelids. "Go and wash in the pool of Siloam," He says.

I have no idea what is going on but His voice has such authority that I immediately do as He asks.

[Imagine yourself in the presence of Jesus and He has given you a command. You don't know why He wants you to do this but you trust Him and do it.]

After I splash water on my eyes and rub the stuff off, I stand up and immediately light floods through my closed lids. What the...! I open my eyes and almost fall over with shock. Sunshine is dazzling me. I can see! I have sight!

I am so excited that I laugh and spin around looking, looking, at colours and shapes and people. Everything!

My neighbours are amazed. They take me to the Pharisees to show me off. As the Pharisees question me, I quickly realize that they are angry that Jesus cured my blindness on this the Sabbath day. Also, they do not believe that I was born blind so they call my parents to verify that. This they do but have no explanation of how I can now see. But my parents don't want any trouble so they tell the Pharisees I am of age to answer questions myself.

The Pharisees ask me yet again how I was cured, but they don't seem to like the answer. They tell me that Jesus is a sinner and not from God and they don't know where He came from. Now, I am an uneducated man but for all their education they don't seem to know much at all. I almost laugh in their faces.

"That is just what is so amazing!" I say. "You don't know where He comes from, yet He has opened my eyes. We know that God doesn't listen to sinners, but God does listen to people who are devout and do His will. Ever since the world began it is unheard of for anyone to open the eyes of someone born blind; if this man were not from God He wouldn't have been able to do anything." With that dose of truth they threw me out but I didn't care.

[Ask yourself if you would have had the same courage in the face of such authoritarian opposition. Do you ever water down your faith to blend in?]

I am very happy when Jesus comes looking for me. "Do you believe in the Son of man," He asks.

I reply, "Sir, tell me who He is so that I may believe in Him."

Jesus says, "You have seen Him; He is speaking to you."

I fall to my knees and worship Him. "Lord, I believe," I say.

[Ask yourself: when was the last time you wholeheartedly worshipped God? Appreciated His majesty? His omnipotence? Bent your head at the name of Jesus? No matter how close we come to God there is generally room for improvement. Make yourself a promise to get on your knees more often to pray at home.]

[Ask Jesus if there is anything He wants to tell you now.]

A witness to the Crucifixion

I wanted to put in a meditation so that you would mentally experience standing at the foot of the Cross and thus appreciate, even more, what Jesus did for us; for you. But as a prefix to that, I want to tell you of a vision my own father had of the Crucifixion. It is something to ponder on.

It happened in January 2005. My father was hospitalized in a collapsed state. It took three days for a diagnosis of sepsis to be made and he survived by a miracle. One night though, before the diagnosis, with my father's life hanging in the balance, he saw a vision of Jesus.

"Jesus was lying on the horizontal cross, not yet nailed," Dad said. "He was struggling to stop His hand being pushed into position on the wooden strut." My father saw two pairs of hands fighting to force this. And he was aware of another person there waiting to hammer in the first nail.

"I saw that Jesus was absolutely human and terrified," said Dad. "He knew that once the first nail went in that would set in motion the whole event from which there was no going back." My father was appalled by what he saw. "I felt so very sorry for Him," he said, clearly deeply moved by the memory.

Here we focus on the account written in the Gospel of John, chapter 19 verses 17 to 30. To help deepen the experience put your whole focus onto this as before as you carry out the following 3-step visualization.

Visualization

Step 1.
Take a deep breath. Breathe out slowly and relax.

Step 2.
Say this prayer.

Prayer for understanding of the bystanders' reactions
Dear Lord Jesus,
Please will You help me to relive the day of Your Crucifixion
so that I see in my mind's eye Your sacrifice for my salvation.
I ask this in Your name Lord and I thank You.

Step 3.
Embark on a journey of discovery by putting yourself in the
place of a spectator of the Crucifixion to understand more fully
the horrific ordeal Jesus went through for you.

I am standing right at the foot of the cross. I am so close that my
hand is on the rough, dry, squared-off post hammered into the
ground. I take a few steps back and with head bent forwards, not
daring to look upwards at my Lord, I listen. The lamentations of
the women beside me and around me fill my ears. My own tears
join their river of sorrow.

None of us is voicing, yet, our incredulity: we never thought
it would come to this. Instead we are filled with grief. Shocked to
the core by the torture and certain death of our beloved Master.

Then a voice pipes up, "Let us not tear it, but cast lots for it to
see whose it shall be." My eyes swivel towards the four soldiers.
One of them is holding Jesus' tunic and they are laughing. I
shake my head, dumfounded by their callous attitude. But then
I realize: for them, this is all in a day's work.

I move back a few more paces to give the family room. In
front of me stands John – one of the disciples, and Jesus' mother.
She is distraught and her sister has a comforting arm around
her waist. On her other side stands Mary the wife of Clopas,
who also has one arm around His mother and the other around
Mary Magdalene.

They all stand staring up at Jesus. I take a deep breath and try to be brave. Slowly, slowly, starting with His feet, so cruelly pinned, my eyes travel upwards past the lash marks visible on His sides – though His poor torn back is hidden – and, finally, I take in the whole terrible picture. My heart almost stops with the brutality of it all. I gaze on His dear face and all the pain is written there.

[Spend a few moments contemplating the fact that Jesus is on the cross writhing in agony so that you can, when your life is done, join Him in Heaven for all eternity.]

I see that Jesus is staring at His mother. Even at this moment it is clear that He wants to alleviate *her* pain. He shifts His gaze to John then pointedly back to Mary. "Woman, this is your son," He says, and to John, "This is your mother." John nods. Mary will be taken care of.

Jesus speaks again. "I am thirsty," He says. And they soak a sponge in sour wine and hold it up to His lips. Oh, how I wish it was cool water but that's all there is at hand. After He drinks Jesus says, "It is accomplished." And bowing His head He dies.

[Spend a few moments in the presence of the crucified Lord. Tell Him how sorry you are that your sins put Him on the cross. Thank Him for His great sacrifice. Ask Jesus if there is anything He wants to tell you now.]

[Put all this into your memory and think about it often so that it will inspire you to more and greater acts of loving kindness in your daily life.]

You may like to record any insights or thoughts, gained from drawing so close to the three biblical events above, in your Spiritual Enrichment notebook. You can continue this record as you read and envisage your own favourite Bible passages.

Section Six Overview

- Cultivate the good habit of regular Bible reading.

- Immerse yourself in the stories for a better understanding of their significance.

- Discovering how the ancient texts relate to you enlivens your own life stories.

Section Seven

Stay as Close to God as Possible

A 5-step Appraisal with God

In Section Three under the heading **At the day's end**, I introduced you to a spiritual development method of quickly mulling your day over with God. I hope that you have embraced that and found it useful. Here we build on the principle.

Search me, O God, and know my heart!
Psalm 139:23

Generally, appraisals are associated with assessments carried out in the workplace to gauge how well people are doing their job. With that in mind, I thought we could do something similar so that you could evaluate, more deeply, where you are in your efforts to be more Christ-like.

Set aside about 30 minutes when you won't be disturbed. Have your Spiritual Enrichment notebook and a pen handy. Write the date at the top of a new page.

Meditation

Step 1.

Sit with your back straight and close your eyes. Exhale fully and take a slow in-breath. Hold it for a few seconds and breathe out and feel tension leaving with it. Then say the following prayer.

Prayer for feedback on the things you do well

Dear Lord,

I want to be a better Christian. I want to be perfect as Jesus challenged me to be. To start this process, I ask that You tell me the things about my life that please You.

I ask this in Jesus' name. Amen.

Now sit for a few minutes in God's company and see if He has anything to tell you in answer to your request.

Jot down any insights that arrive.

Step 2.
Take a deep breath. Breathe out slowly and relax again. Then say the following prayer.

Prayer for feedback on the times you don't do well
Dear Lord,
Though I try hard to do Your will, sometimes I get it wrong. So, I ask that You tell me the things about my life that displease You.
I ask this in Jesus' name. Amen.

Now sit for a few minutes in God's company and see if He has anything to tell you in answer to your request.

Jot down any insights that arrive.

Step 3.
Take a deep breath. Breathe out slowly and relax again. Then say the following prayer.

Prayer for guidance on ways to improve
Dear Lord,
I want to please You always. So, I ask You to tell me some ways through which to please You more.
I ask this in Jesus' name. Amen.

Now sit for a few minutes in God's company and see if He has anything to tell you in answer to your request.

Jot down any insights that arrive.

Step 4.
Take a deep breath. Breathe out slowly and relax again. Then
say the following prayer.

Prayer for advice

Dear Lord,
I know that You are Love so I ask that You tell me how to be
more loving in all situations in my life, and so draw even
closer in relationship with You.
I ask this in Jesus' name. Amen.

Now sit for a few minutes in God's company and see if He has
anything to tell you in answer to your request.

Jot down any insights that arrive.

Step 5.
When you have completed the 4 steps above, spend a little more
time looking over what you have written. Then write down
anything relevant that comes to mind. Perhaps you may like to
note how you felt during the prayers. And how you feel now.

No matter what answers did or did not arrive keep open, in
the coming days, to get more insights into the way you live your
life. And the ways you can become more Christ-like. Add these
to your notes and look at them regularly.

When you do another appraisal session with God these notes
may show the progress you have made and also the areas you
may want to pay more attention to in order to please Him more.

Section Seven Overview

- Scheduling regular evaluating heart-to-hearts with God
  keeps your faith growing.

Putting it All Together

Thinking back to the start of this new spiritual journey you see that your quality of life has greatly improved.

Acknowledging the constant presence of the Holy Spirit within you has banished much of the fear and loneliness that earthly tests can bring.

Now that you invite God into every aspect of your life your deepening relationship with Him enriches every aspect of who you are.

- You now create opportunities for Christ to communicate with you when He wants to.

- You use quick heartfelt prayers throughout the day to keep God engaged in your activities.

- When confronted by challenges you invite God's insights and help.

- You bring your faith into your daily life to keep on the track of love.

- You read the Bible regularly and engage with the ancient wisdoms and events in a fresh way.

- You ask God for feedback on your choices so you are able to refine them.

Rolled together this means that, as you no longer only talk to Christ at certain times of the day, you no longer leave Him out in the cold. And, as you invite God's input on *everything*, you are filled with the confidence and joy which come from knowing that you carry out His will in your life.

Inner peace and joy flow freely as you humbly remember that all you have comes from God – starting with the majestic gifts of life and faith. Also, you have moved much nearer to the sometimes daunting goal that Jesus set you: a life of continuous prayer.

Rejoice always, pray constantly, give thanks in all circumstances; for this is the will of God in Christ Jesus for you.
1 Thessalonians 5.16–17

As you continue your spiritual journey, experiencing the fulfilment and joy that come from heart-to-heart communication with God, may you be filled with every blessing! I ask this in the name of Jesus Christ our Lord. Amen.

Teresa O'Driscoll

Author Biography

Born and raised in Cardiff, capital of Wales, Teresa spent a number of years in Athens, capital of Greece, working as a journalist and editor. It was there that she was inspired, by the natural beauty of the country, and the fervour of the people – both in the Catholic cathedral of St Denis where she worshipped and sang in the choir, and of her many Greek Orthodox friends – to write *9 Days to Heaven: How to Make Everlasting Meaning of Your Life*. Now back in her native city she runs writing and spiritual growth workshops, as well as beavering away at her own writing.

In Covid-19 lockdown she was kept sane by channelling the mishmash of emotions into writing. This led to having two books accepted for publication by John Hunt Publications Ltd. So, as well as this one, her debut novel *Angel at the Paradise Hotel* will be released shortly.

Other Books by the Author

Previous title
Non fiction

9 Days to Heaven: How to Make Everlasting Meaning of Your Life, O Books, book and e-book – Christian inspirational programme which uses nature and the senses for a back-to-basics examination of your faith in the company of God. This brings a new, life-enhancing perspective as you see yourself squarely in the context of Eternity.

This book is for people who do not yet know Christ, as well as those who want to know Him better. A simple and practical guide to joyful living.

Readers around the world have shared that it has helped them through very tough times; on occasion acting as a lifeline. Others say it has enriched their life as it helped to deepen their relationship with Christ. Many also say that the enjoyable programme reduces stress levels considerably.

You can read more of this on Teresa's website: http://www.teresaodriscoll.co.uk

"A wonderfully simple yet powerful way to reach what monks and mystics have sought for centuries: a deep, one-on-one communion with God."
John Backman, author of *Why Can't We Talk? Christian Wisdom on Dialogue as a Habit of the Heart*

Upcoming title
Debut novel

Angel at the Paradise Hotel: Because even on vacation personal demons tag along, book and e-book to be published by Roundfire Books – Glimpse the angelic backstory of life as an idyllic Greek resort is visited by evil.

Set on the green and beautiful island of Corfu, when tourism transforms a fishing village, old hatreds, envy, and greed threaten to tear the local community apart. Behind the scenes personal demons fuel division while guardian angels battle to neutralize their influence.

Follow the action as hotelier Jason, planning to get rich, ruthlessly chases his goal, unaware of the trouble and danger he is stirring up. Three visitors from Ireland, America and Wales bring their own problems. Clare, running from a broken relationship, is drawn into a love triangle with Jason. Aeron, battling a mid-life crisis is closer to despair than he realizes. While Bethany, jolted by a Big Birthday into doing a Shirley Valentine, is hoping it will sort her life out.

As the sizzling summer unfolds each faces make or break challenges. Extra help is at hand though, with the arrival of Gabriella, angel of Greece. When meddling demons prevail, and smouldering greed and vengeance reach flashpoint, can she avert disaster?

A note from the author

Thank you for reading my book *Pray Then Listen: A Heart-to-Heart with God*. I hope so much that you have found it useful. If you have a few moments, please feel free to add your review to your favourite online sites for feedback. Also, I would really like to hear your comments on this and my other books so please get in touch with me through my website https://www.teresaodriscoll.co.uk

You can follow my blogs with the link on my website homepage.

God bless, Teresa O'Driscoll

CIRCLE
BOOKS

CHRISTIAN FAITH

Circle Books explores a wide range of disciplines within the field of Christian faith and practice. It also draws on personal testimony and new ways of finding and expressing God's presence in the world today.

If you have enjoyed this book, why not tell other readers by posting a review on your preferred book site. Recent bestsellers from Circle Books are:

I Am With You (Paperback)
John Woolley

These words of divine encouragement were given to John Woolley in his work as a hospital chaplain, and have since inspired and uplifted tens of thousands, even changed their lives.

Paperback: 978-1-90381-699-8 ebook: 978-1-78099-485-7

God Calling
A. J. Russell

365 messages of encouragement channelled from Christ to two anonymous "Listeners".

Hardcover: 978-1-905047-42-0 ebook: 978-1-78099-486-4